Mind-Boggling
WORD
PUZZLES

MARTIN GARDNER
Illustrated by V.G Myers

Sterling Publishing Co., Inc.
New York

For Marilyn vos Savant,

A maven who can't fail to write gracefully about
anything from word puzzles to psychology,
and how to spell *hippopotamus* and *paleontology.*
— A clerihew by Armand T. Ringer

Library of Congress Cataloging-in-Publication Data

Gardner, Martin, 1914–
  Mind-boggling word puzzles/Martin Gardner; illustrated by
V.G. Myers.
        p. cm
  Includes index.
  ISBN 0-8069-3690-8
   1. Word games–Juvenile literature. 2. Puzzles–Juvenile
literature.[1. Word games. 2. Puzzles.] I. Myers, V.G., ill. II. Title.

GV1507.W8 G37 2001
793.73–dc21

                                        2001020195

Published by Sterling Publishing Company, Inc.
387 Park Avenue South, New York, N.Y. 10016
© 2001 by Martin Gardner
Distributed in Canada by Sterling Publishing
C/o Canadian Manda Group, One Atlantic Avenue, Suite 105
Toronto, Ontario, Canada M6K 3E7
Distributed in Great Britain and Europe by Chris Lloyd
463 Ashley Road, Parkstone, Poole, Dorset, BH14 0AX, England
Distributed in Australia by Capricorn Link (Australia) Pty Ltd.
P.O. Box 6651, Baulkham Hills, Business Centre, NSW 2153,
Australia

Contents

foreword

Hundreds of puzzle books have been published over the last few decades, many of the best by Sterling. It is surprising how often old puzzles keep appearing over and over again in most puzzle books, only slightly altered by different story lines. The word and letter puzzles here, with few exceptions, are unfamiliar ones — not to be found in other collections. Many are original. Some I found in old and new periodicals. Some were sent to me by friends.

It goes without saying that you'll enjoy these brainteasers more if you can refrain from peeking at the answers until you've done your best to solve each one.

1. Warm-ups

1. William's Preferences

William likes apples better than oranges, and vanilla
ice cream better than chocolate. He would rather
watch a baseball or football game on TV than hockey,
enjoys summer and fall more than spring and winter,
thinks *Newsweek* a better magazine than *Time*, and is
convinced that *High Noon* is a greater Western movie
than *Destry Rides Again*.

Can you explain why William has these
preferences?

Answer on page 83.

2. The IDK Band

Six college students, all musicians, decided to form a rock band that they named the IDKers. The group consisted of five men and a lead singer named Matilda, who was tall and had red hair. The men were all from New Jersey, but Matilda came to the college from New York.

When members of the band were asked what IDK stood for, they agreed that they would always answer, "I don't know." Can you guess why they said this?

Answer on page 83.

3. Snowballs

"A snowball sentence," said Mr. Jones to his daughter, "is one in which each word is one letter longer than the preceding word. Do you think you can construct such a sentence?"

The daughter thought for several minutes before she said, "I am not that smart, father."

Prove that the daughter was smarter than she said she was.

Answer on page 83.

4. Name the Month

What month is indicated by these strange symbols?

Answer on page 83.

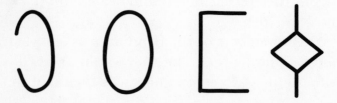

5. Wrong Caption

Professor Letterman, who teaches English at Wordsmith College, has just hired Miss Jones, his new assistant.

The caption seems not to fit the picture. You can make it fit by changing one letter.

Answer on page 83.

6. A Tennis Player

What is this tennis player saying?

Answer on page 83.

7. Four Suits

I _____ my dog.
I _____ my cat.
I carry a _____ .
I would love to own a _____ mine.

If you were to insert in the blanks a symbol for each of the four playing-card suits, each line would make sense.

Answer on page 83.

8. Name the Student

I DID THIS SUM

2856104
4454913
_____
7311017

WHAT IS
MY NAME?

The sum on the blackboard is correct. Can you find in the picture the first name of the student?

Answer on page 83.

9. What Letter?

This is a picture of a letter. Can you decide what letter it is?

Answer on page 83.

10. The Sad King

King are you sorry you are King?

What's so remarkable about the caption below the picture?

Answer on page 84.

11. A Short Teaser

There is a familiar word of five letters that becomes shorter if you add two letters to it. What's the word?

Answer on page 84.

12. Name the Book

In what book are the months listed with April appearing first and September appearing last?

Answer on page 84.

13. Where?

There is a familiar saying that lists all the months, with September coming first and February last. What saying is it?

Answer on page 84.

14. The Two Doors

The words on the two doors seem to be written in a strange script. See if you can translate them into English without adding any words to the page. There is a ridiculously easy way to read the two words.

Answer on page 84.

2. Family Talk

15. The Palindrome Family

Here you see a drawing based on a photograph of Blake de Kalb, his wife the former Norah Sharon, their three children, and their young dog, Otto.

Your task is to identify each person and the pet with a three-letter word that is a palindrome — a word that spells the same in both directions, like the name of the parents and the dog. For example, the three-letter palindrome for the dog would be PUP.

What kind of car does the family own?

And at what time of day was the picture taken?

Answer on page 84.

16. Name the Girl

Mary's father has three daughters. The oldest is named April. The second oldest is named May. What's the first name of the youngest daughter?

Answer on page 84.

17. Three Sisters

There are three blond sisters named Dinah, Betty, and Marilyn. Of the three, only Dinah might dye her hair red.

Concealed in the two previous sentences is something that could explode. Can you find it?

Answer on page 84.

18. How Many Cookies?

Jim 81, Joan 812

Jim and his sister Joan discovered a jar of cookies in a kitchen cupboard.

1. Can you interpret the picture's caption?

2. If the jar contained 10 cookies, and Jim and Joan ate all but three, how many cookies would be left in the jar?

Answer on page 84.

19. Stop and Snap

Mrs. Rendrag and her son Nitram had finished washing and drying the dinner dishes.

"Now that the dishes are done," said Mrs. Rendrag, "let's do the STOP AND SNAP."

The words STOP and SNAP don't make sense. Do you see how a simple change of their letters will let you know what Mrs. Rendrag actually said to her son?

After you have solved this puzzle, you should have no difficulty learning the real names of Mrs. Rendrag and Nitram.

Answer on page 84.

20. Tommy's Tumble

Little Tommy fell off his tricycle and bumped his head so hard that he was knocked unconscious. When he came to, he spoke perfect French. How come?

Answer on page 85.

21. How Many Peaches?

Joy's father brought a paper sack home from the supermarket. It contained a certain number of peaches.

Joy took no peaches from the sack, and she left no peaches in the sack.

How many peaches were inside the sack?

Answer on page 85.

22.
A Baby Crossword

1	4	5
2		
3		

Across
1. Uncle ____
2. Cherry ____
3. Fine ____

Down
1. Health ____
2. Fresh ____
3. Have we ____?

If you solve this easy 3 x 3 crossword puzzle, you'll find that in addition to the horizontal and vertical words, each diagonal provides two other words. It is not known whether such a word square, with eight different common English words, can be made without duplicating at least one letter.

Answer on page 85.

3. What Did You Say?

23. What's the Question?

The clerk in the railroad station is responding to the lady's question. Can you guess what she has just asked him?

Answer on page 85.

24. Crazy Words

Professor Letterman is holding a sheet on which he lettered what he claims are seven common English words.

It's easy to find out what the words are if you perform a simple operation. What must you do?

ZO—ZO   OON

ZOOZ   ZCZ

ZO—N   ZO—ZC

X—Z

Answer on page 85.

25. Day's End

Is it true that *day* begins with d and *ends* with e?

Answer on page 85.

26. Lisping Verse

"You can't," says Tom to lisping Bill,
"Find any rhyme for month."
"You are wrong," was Bill's reply.
"I'll find a rhyme at _____."

Answer on page 85.

27. In the Middle

Professor Letterman claims that P is the middle letter of the alphabet. How can he be right?

Answer on page 85.

28. A Missing Letter

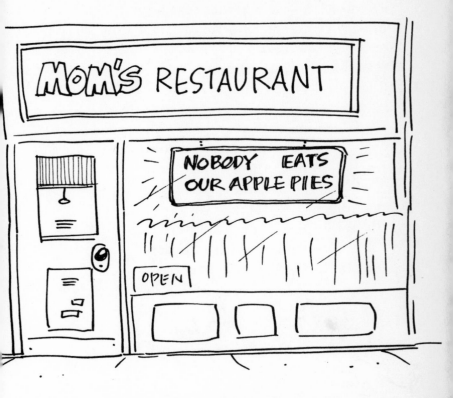

An electric sign in the window of Mom's Restaurant is missing a letter. What letter is it?

Answer on page 85.

29. A Missing Word

In each of the eight sentences below, there is a word missing. Professor Letterman says it's the same word in all eight places.

Can you supply the one word that makes sense of each sentence?

____ I hit him in the eye yesterday.
I ____ hit him in the eye yesterday.
I hit ____ him in the eye yesterday.
I hit him ____ in the eye yesterday.
I hit him in ____ the eye yesterday.
I hit him in the ____ eye yesterday.
I hit him in the eye ____ yesterday.
I hit him in the eye yesterday ____.

Answer on page 86.

30. A Puzzling Door

What in the world do these strange words on the door mean?

Answer on page 86.

31. Correct the Spellings

I BIND ON SHE HANK IT FORTH TOO IS THY BUST.

If you change one letter in each word, it will make a sentence that is a well-known proverb.

Answer on page 86.

32. SH!

Is there another common English word, aside from SUGAR, in which S, as the first letter, is pronounced SH? Can you name it?

Answer on page 86.

33. Four Arrows

Each arrow points to a word. If you rearrange the letters properly in each word, the picture will make sense.

Answer on page 86.

34. Three-Letter Words

In this sentence there are neither more nor less than ___ words with three letters. What can you put in the blank space to make the sentence correct?

Answer on page 86.

35. WYKMIITY and WYLTK

When Susan asked Tom what the letters on his T-shirt meant, his reply was, "Will you kiss me if I tell you?" After Susan kissed him, Tom explained the letters. Tom then asked Susan what *her* letters meant. See if you can figure out what the letters stand for on both T-shirts.

Answer on page 86.

36. ACE GIK MOQ SUWY

What is the basis for the sequence of strange three-letter words printed above?

Answer on page 86.

37. What Is Santa Saying?

Can you figure out what this department store Santa Claus is saying to the little girl who has just climbed onto his lap?

Answer on page 86.

38. A Yuletide Rebus

The picture represents a line from a well-known Christmas song. Can you guess the line?

Answer on page 87.

39. Three Students

At a party at Wordsmith College, three students were asked to pin their first names on their clothes. Instead of names, it looks as if these three wrote down numbers instead.

Can you guess their first names?

Answer on page 87.

40. Ruth's Cipher

Ruth numbered the letters of the alphabet as follows:

    A = 1

    B = 2

    C = 3

and so on to Z = 26.

She sent the following code message to her friend:

91215225251521

Can you decode it?

Answer on page 87.

4. Creatures

41. Monkey Talk

IWNTBNN

1. This clever monkey has been taught how to speak. To learn what she is saying, insert the same letter five times in the letter sequence shown.

2. After you have solved this puzzle, see if you can insert the same letter four times in LBM to learn where the monkey is living in a zoo, *Alabama*

3. And insert the same letter three times in BRBR to learn the monkey's name.

Barbara

Answer on page 87.

42. Concealed Creatures

Does the pigeon want to catch the butterfly?

The word "pig" is hidden inside the word "pigeon." Can you find the names of four other creatures concealed in the sentence above?

Answer on page 87.

43. A Horse Jingle

I was a racehorse.
2 was 12.
111 race.
2112.

Can you make sense of this poem?

Answer on page 87.

44. Spell the Creature

Y	Q	U	W	M
T	S	I	F	E
R	H	L	D	N
A	P	O	G	V
B	K	C	X	Z

Put your finger on a letter in the square. By moving the finger left, right, up, or down — but never diagonally — from one square to one next to it, see if you can spell a familiar seven-letter word that stands for a living creature.

Answer on page 87.

45. Nagging Question

Can you think of an animal whose name begins with N?

Answer on page 87.

46. A Freezing Frog

This poor frog is freezing on a cold winter day. The words FROG and COLD are closely related by the positions of their letters in the alphabet. Can you determine how they are related?

Answer on page 87.

47. Three Bunnies

Why are these three rabbits called the three musketeers?

Answer on page 88.

48. Old Mother Hubbard

Old Mother Hubbard
Went to the cupboard
   To get her poor dog a bone,
But when she got there,
The cupboard was bare,
   And so her poor dog had none.

Professor Letterman says that word-play buffs find something very strange about this old nursery rhyme. Can you determine what it is?

Answer on page 88.

49. Name the Poodle

What's the name of Mrs. Letterman's poodle.

Answer on page 88.

50. Where's the Comma?

Did you see the lion eating Herman?

Actually, Herman was not injured by the lion. See if you can place a comma in the above sentence to make it read properly.

Answer on page 88.

5. Getting It Right

51. Who Does What?

On the left are the first names of sixteen women.
On the right is a list of sixteen professions. Each
woman has one of these jobs. For example, Sue is a
lawyer.

See if you can match each name on the left with
the related profession on the right.

Sue	Chiropractor
Grace	Waitress
Bridget	Upholsterer
Patience	Engineer
Carlotta	Dancer
Robin	Thief
Ophelia	Physician
Wanda	Milliner
Sophie	Minister
Hattie	Singer
Octavia	Magician
Carrie	Gambler
Betty	Musician
Carol	Used car salesman
Faith	Jeweler
Pearl	Lawyer

Answer on page 88.

52. Name the Time

See if you can guess the correct times for the following situations:

1. A tiger ate a postman. Let P.M. be an abbreviation for a man who delivers mail. What time is it?

2. What time is it when you have a severe toothache?

3. Three cats are chasing a mouse. What time is it?

4. If your antique clock struck thirteen times, what time would it be?

Answer on page 88.

53. Spell a Name

The six shapes shown here have been cut from cardboard. Can you rearrange them to spell a girl's name?

Answer on page 89.

54. A Ribbon Loop

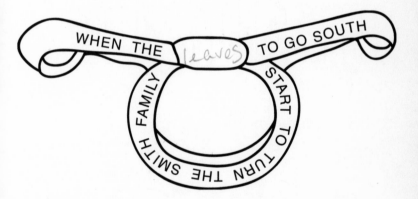

WHEN THE *leaves* TO GO SOUTH START TO TURN THE SMITH FAMILY

Put a word in the blank space so that the sentence makes sense when you read it around the loop.

Answer on page 89.

55. A Puzzling Landscape

Somewhere in the above scene there is something with a name that begins with S. What is it?

Answer on page 89.

56. Guess the Pseudonym

Armand T. Ringer is an anagram of the name of a writer with whom you are familiar. Who is he or she?

Answer on page 89.

57. An Ode to Apricots

Janet bought some stewed apricots on a cold
    February morning for her three children,
Mary, Julie, and Junior.
    Apricots are delicious when stewed.
Maybe you don't think so?
    Junior doesn't like stewed apricots, but
Julie and Mary believe that they
    Augment the taste of cereals and ice cream.
Separately, stewed apricots are also tasty.
    Octopuses would surely find apricots a
Novel kind of fruit, but they might
    Decline to eat an apricot once they tasted it.

This peculiar free-verse poem by Armand T. Ringer
has something remarkable about each line. Can you
discover what it is?

Answer on page 89.

58. Fill the Blank

In this square
there are _____
e's.

What number word from 1 to 10 would make the
statement in the sign accurate?

Answer on page 89.

59. Do You Deny It?

No expert on word play can deny that there is a familiar English word of four letters that ends in ENY. What is it?

deny

Answer on page 89.

60. Where to Draw the Lines?

By adding slash marks between the letters of HESITATE like this:

HE/SIT/ATE

you can make three words. Now see if you can add six slashes to INDISCRIMINATION to make seven common words.

Answer on page 89.

61. He! He!

Can you name a common word that starts and ends with HE?

Can you name a common word that contains the letters ADAC in that order? It may give you a headache to answer both questions!

Answer on page 89.

headache

62. Guess the Punchlines

This is a test of your ability to make jokes. Each opening remark is followed by a funny punchline. Try to supply the missing line before you check the answers.

1. FATHER: The man who marries my daughter will get a prize.
   BOYFRIEND: _____

2. WOMAN (*in restaurant*): Is there soup on the menu?
   WAITER: _____

3. TEACHER: Where was the Declaration of Independence signed?
   STUDENT: _____

4. JUDGE: Order! Order in the court!
   PRISONER: _____

5. WOMAN (*to psychiatrist*): I need help. Nobody pays any attention to me. I feel like I'm invisible.
   PSYCHIATRIST: _____

6. PATIENT (*after a physical examination*): How do I stand?
   DOCTOR: _____

7. PSYCHIATRIST: Do you have trouble making up your mind?
   PATIENT: _____

Answer on page 89.

63. The Wrong Words

A man who couldn't read English was attending a convention in the United States. He asked a friend to tell him how to distinguish the men's washroom from the women's.

"It's easy," said the friend. "Just go to the room that has the shortest word on its door."

The man did as he was told, but found himself inside a washroom with a bunch of screaming ladies. How come?

Answer on page 90.

64. A Typewriter Teaser

Using only the letters on the second line of the typewriter or computer keyboard, see if you can spell a familiar ten-letter word.

Answer on page 90.

65. Professor Letterman's Revenge

MR. LETTERMAN WILL BE
UNABLE TO MEET HIS
CLASSES TODAY.

Because of his wife's sudden illness, Professor Letterman wrote on the blackboard, "Mr. Letterman will be unable to meet his classes today."

As he left the room, a student approached the blackboard and erased the first letter of "classes." Everybody laughed.

The professor turned around, walked back to the blackboard, and erased another letter. What letter did he erase?

Answer on page 90.

66. The Marrying Bachelor

Tim Rines is a respected bachelor in this hometown, even though he married more than fifty ladies who live there. Rearrange the letters of his name to spell his profession.

Now rearrange the letters of PEPSI-COLA to spell the name that goes in the blank of "The First _____ Church," where you will find Mr. Rines every Sunday morning.

Answer on page 90.

episcopal

67. HIJKLMNO

The letters above, when properly understood, stand for a common liquid. Name it.

Answer on page 90.

68. An Unusual Word

Can you think of a familiar word with three U's in it?

Answer on page 90.

6. What Do You Have in Mind?

69. A Clock Conundrum

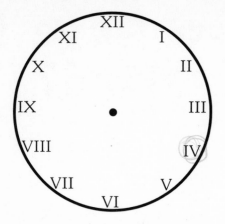

Clocks often use Roman numerals for the hours. When Walter B. Gibson, the writer who created *The Shadow* and wrote many books about magic, was seven, he sent a letter to *St. Nicholas*, a magazine for children. In the letter, which the magazine published, he asked which Roman numeral on a clock suggested the name of a common plant. What did Walter have in mind?

Answer on page 90.

70. Ten Body Parts

Many parts of the human body have three-letter names, for example, "arm." See if you can think of at least nine others.

Answer on page 90.

71. Opposites

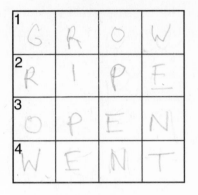

1. shrink
2. green
3. shut
4. came

On this simple crossword puzzle, put words that are the opposite of the definitions given. If you do it correctly, the result will be a word square with the same words vertically as horizontally.

Answer on page 90.

72. ERGRO

Put three letters in front of ERGRO, and the same three letters at the end of ERGRO, to make an 11-letter word that tells you where all the world's oil comes from.

Answer on page 90.

73. One-Letter Captions

Under each of the eight pictures, place a single letter that describes the picture. For example, the letter J describes the picture of a Jay. The last picture tells you to look in a mirror.

Answer on page 90.

74. The Annoyed Sign Painter

The owner of the Bell Yacht Company refused to pay the sign painter because he put the words Bell and Yacht too close together.

Late that night the annoyed sign painter returned and changed one letter on the door to indicate how he felt. What letter did he change?

Answer on page 91.

75. Fold and Cut

A	B
C	D
E	F
G	H

Fold a sheet of paper so that when you open it flat the creases will form eight rectangles. Write in these boxes the first eight letters of the alphabet in order, as shown above.

Now fold the sheet along the creases in any manner you like to make a packet with the eight rectangles together, like the leaves of a book. With scissors, trim away all four edges of the packet. This will leave you with eight separate paper rectangles.

Spread the eight pieces on the table. Four letters will be faceup and four facedown. Try to form a word with the faceup letters. If you can't make a word, turn the pieces over and try again with the other four letters.

What word did you form?

Answer on page 91.

76. In and Out

BANK

ENTER

EXIT

Add a letter to one of the three words in the picture to make a new word that fits the blank space in each of the following three sentences:

1. Do unicorns _exist_?
2. He had a _blank_ expression on his face.
3. H is the _____ of nothing.

Answer on page 91.

77. From Z to A

The alphabet goes from A to Z. What goes from Z to A?

Answer on page 91.

78. What Can It Be?

Luke had it before. Paul had it behind. Matthew never had it. Girls have it once. Boys can't have it. Mrs. Mulligan had it twice. Mr. Lowell had it once before and twice after.
    What is it?

Answer on page 91.

79. Number Anagram

Arrange the nine letters of "extension" to spell the names of three numbers, each less than 20.

Answer on page 91.

7. Toughies

80. ENINYOS

Can you add the same letter at four different spots in
ENINYOS to make an appropriate caption for the
illustration?

Answer on page 91.

81. Name the Painting

"No hat, a smile," describes a famous painting. If you
rearrange the letters, they will spell the name of the
painting. What picture is it?

Answer on page 91.

82. The Locked Safe

You see here the three dials of a safe. To open the safe, you must rotate the dials until a familiar six-letter word can be read horizontally, like the letters TUYCNO in the illustration.

What word opens the safe?

Answer on page 91.

83. Change the Sign

A sign by a lake says:

A group of children cleverly added punctuation to the sign that allowed them to go swimming. How did they do this?

Answer on page 91.

84. Three B's

The words "bubble" and "babble" each contain three B's. Professor Letterman created a hubbub in his classroom when he offered a prize to the first student who could think of a word that had three B's, but which didn't begin with a B. What's the word?

Answer on page 91.

85. Horace Spencer

"MY NAME, GOOD SIR, IS HORACE SPENCER. MY AGE TWELVE YEARS, HEIGHT FOUR FEET _____."

Can you complete the second line of what Horace is saying so that it rhymes with the first line?

Answer on page 92.

86. What's the Number?

The word FORTY is the only number-word with its letters in alphabetical order. What number-word has its letters in *reverse* alphabetical order? *Hint:* It's less than fifty.

Answer on page 92.

87. NY, PA, AND OZ

L. Frank Baum, who wrote fourteen Oz books, was born and raised in New York. Ruth Plumly Thompson, who continued the Oz series after Baum died, lived in Pennsylvania.

There are close word-play associations between the words OZ and NY, and OZ and PA. Do you see how OZ is connected to the two state abbreviations?

Answer on page 92.

88. Curious Cards

Mr. Curio owns an antiques shop by the side of the road. When his store is open, he puts four large cards side by side on the window ledge. They bear the letters O-P-E-N.

When he is away, he rearranges the cards to spell a word that tells visitors his store is closed.

How does he alter the letters?

Answer on page 92.

89. GHGHGH

Professor Letterman is explaining to his class how to pronounce the word *ghghgh*.

"The first *gh*," he says, "is pronounced the same way as *gh* in *hiccough*. The second *gh* is pronounced like the *gh* in *Edinburgh*. And the third *gh* has the sound of *gh* in *laugh*."

If you pronounce all three *gh*'s the way the professor says, what word does it make?

Answer on page 92.

90. HAL and IBM

HAL is the name of a supercomputer on the spaceship featured in the movie version of Arthur Clarke's famous novel *2001*. IBM is the name of a company that makes computers.

There is a curious relationship between HAL and IBM. Can you discover it?

Answer on page 92.

91. Ten Flying Saucers

"Have you ever seen a UFO?" I asked Professor Letterman.

"Indeed I have," he replied. "I've seen ten."

Then he added, "I'm only kidding. But here's a word puzzle for you. What operation can you perform on TEN that will change the word to UFO?

Answer on page 92.

92. Kubla Khan

In Xanadu did Kubla Khan
A stately pleasure dome decree;
Where Alph, the sacred river, ran
Through caverns measureless to man
Down to a sunless sea.

One of Samuel Taylor Coleridge's most famous
poems begins with the five lines quoted above. Do
you see what is so remarkable about them?

Answer on page 92.

93. Merry Christmas

A merry Christmas and a happy new year!

Merry, merry carols you'll have sung us,
Christmas remains Christmas even when you are not
  here,
And though afar and lonely, you're among us.
A bond is there, a bond at times near broken.
Happy be Christmas then, when happy, clear,
New heart-warm links are forged, new ties betoken
Year ripe with loving giving birth to year.

This poem, by the late British poet J.A. Lindon, has a
truly amazing structure. Can you figure out what it is?

Answer on page 92.

94. Two Words

We __x__ on the __y__ way,
And we __y__ on the __x__ way.

Fill out the two sentences by putting a five-letter word in the blanks marked x, and a four-letter word in the blanks marked y.

Answer on page 93.

95. Blind Bus Driver

A newspaper headline reads, "Blind Man Is Hired to Drive School Bus."

How can this be true? If you interpret the sentence properly, it will make good sense.

Answer on page 93.

96. A Lewis Carroll Puzzle

The first nine letters of the alphabet are A B C D E F G H I. Cross out the H. Can you arrange the remaining eight letters to make two words that accurately describe the clown?

Answer on page 93.

97. A Curious Sequence

What is the next pair of letters in this sequence? ST ND RD TH __?

Answer on page 93.

98. Name Two

Three common English words begin with DW. Can you name at least two?

Answer on page 93.

99. Decode a Number

Each letter in ABCDEFGHIJ, the first ten letters of the alphabet, stands for a different digit in a number that is less than 100. There is only one answer. What's the number?

Answer on page 93.

100. Miles and Miles

Name four words that have a mile between their first and last letters.

Answer on page 93.

101. After AB

What letter in the alphabet comes after AB?

Answer on page 93.

102.
Add a Line

Can you draw a short line on
       A   B   C   D   E
to turn it into a five-letter word?

Answer on page 93.

103. DNE EHT

YAD DOO GAE VAH

Answer on page 93.

ANSWERS

1. William's Preferences

William, whose name has a double letter, likes things with double letters in their names. (Thanks to Marilyn vos Savant.)

2. The IDK Band

IDK are the initial letters of "I don't know."

3. Snowballs

The daughter spoke a snowball sentence.

4. Name the Month

Cover the top halves of each symbol and you will see the word JULY.

5. Wrong Caption

Change hired to fired.

6. A Tennis Player

"Tennis, anyone?"

7. Four Suits

The symbols in order are Heart, Spade, Club, and Diamond.

8. Name the Student

Turn the page upside down and you'll see the sum turn into LIONEL.

9. What Letter?

Give the page a quarter turn counterclockwise. Do you see the letter E?

10. The Sad King
It's a word palindrome. the words read the same left to right and right to left.

11. A Short Teaser
Short.

12. Name the Book
In a dictionary.

13. Where?
The mnemonic that begins "Thirty days hath September..." (Thanks to Sol Golomb.)

14. The Two Doors
Hold the page upside down in front of a mirror.

15. The Palindrome Family
The three-letter words are POP (or DAD), MOM, BOB, SIS, TOT, and PUP. The family owns A TOYOTA, and the photo was taken at NOON. When Bob first saw their brand-new Toyota, he shouted, "WOW!"

16. Name the Girl
Mary.

17. Three Sisters
Dynamite (Dinah might).

18. How Many Cookies
1. Jim ate one, Joan ate one two.
2. If the children ate all but three, then three would be left.

19. Stop and Snap
"Let's do the POTS and PANS (STOP and SNAP backwards)," said Mrs. Gardner to her son Martin.

20. Tommy's Tumble
Tommy and his parents lived in France.

21. How Many Peaches?
There were two peaches in the sack. Joy took one of them out of the sack. To take one peach (singular) is not to take peaches (plural) and to leave one peach is not to leave peaches.

22. A Baby Crossword

S	A	M
P	I	E
A	R	T

23. What's the Question?
The lady has asked the clerk how long her train will be in the station. His answer is from: "Two to 2:00, to 2:22."

24. Crazy Words
The professor is holding the sheet by the wrong edge. Give the sheet (page) a quarter turn counterclockwise and read the words vertically.

25. Day's End
Yes, *day* starts with d, and *ends* starts with e.

26. Lisping Verse
The missing word is "wunth."

27. In the Middle
P is the middle letter of "the alphabet."

28. A Missing Letter
The missing letter is B, the first letter of BEATS. When my wife Charlotte checked this puzzle, she supplied three other answers: Nobody *heats* our apple pies; Nobody eats *sour* apple pies; and Nobody eats *four* apple pies.

29. A Missing Word
The word is "only."

30. A Puzzling Door
Divided properly, the letters spell "To open door, push."

31. Correct the Spellings
The proverb is illustrated by the picture. A bird in the hand is worth two in the bush.

32. SH!
Sure.

33. Four Arrows
The words are anagrams of NORTH, SOUTH, EAST, and WEST. I found this puzzle in Marilyn vos Savant's popular *Parade* column.

34. Three-Letter Words
You can't put *two*, because then the sentence would have three three-letter words. So you must put the numeral 2.

35. WYKMIITY and WYLTK
Tom's letters are the initials of "Will you kiss me if I tell you?" and Susan's letters are the first letters of "Wouldn't you like to know?"

36. ACE GIK MOQ SUWY
They are the letters at odd positions (1, 3, 5, 7...) in the alphabet. Note the remarkable fact that all five vowels, AEIOU, and the sometime vowel Y, are included in the sequence.

37. What Is Santa Saying?
Read aloud the words Santa is speaking. They will spell the letters of MERRY CHRISTMAS. (Thanks to Mike Steuben.)

38. A Yuletide Rebus
Silent night (knight), holy (holey) night (knight). (Thanks to Dexter Cleveland, who put this on his Christmas card.)

39. Three Students
The students made the mistake of pinning their names upside down. Turn the page around to read the names: OLLIE, ELSIE, and LESLIE.

40. Ruth's Cipher
If you divide the numbers like this: 9/12/15/22/5/25/15/21, the message decodes as "I LOVE YOU."

41. Monkey Talk
The monkey is saying, "I want a banana." Her name is Barbara, and the zoo is in Alabama. "I know how to spell banana," a little girl once said, "but I never know when to stop."

42. Concealed Creatures
Doe, ant, cat, fly.

43. A Horse Jingle
One and two are the names of two racehorses. The poem reads:

> One was a racehorse.
> Two was one, too.
> One won one race.
> Two won one, too.

44. Spell the Creature
Goldfish. (Thanks to Charles Bostick.)

45. Nagging Question
Nag. And also, a less nagging answer, narwhal (a kind of whale).

46. A Freezing Frog
Shift each letter of COLD ahead three steps in the alphabet. You arrive at FROG.

47. Three Bunnies

They must get "ears."

48. Old Mother Hubbard

The nursery rhyme is missing the vowel "i."

49. Name the Poodle

Did you notice that there was no question mark after the brain-teaser's statement? The name of the poodle is "What."

50. Where's the Comma?

Did you see the lion eating, Herman?

51. Who Does What?

Sue — lawyer
Grace — dancer
Bridget — engineer
Patience — physician
Carlotta — used car salesman
Robin — thief
Ophelia — chiropractor
Wanda — magician
Sophie — upholsterer
Hattie — milliner
Octavia — musician
Carrie — waitress
Betty — gambler
Carol — singer
Faith — minister
Pearl — jeweler

52. Name the Time

1. 8 (ate) P.M.
2. 2:30 (tooth hurty).
3. Three after one.
4. Time to get the clock fixed.

53. Spell a Name
MARCIA.

54. A Ribbon Loop
The word is *leaves*.

55. A Puzzling Landscape
Sky.

56. Guess the Pseudonym
Martin Gardner.

57. An Ode to Apricots
The first three letters of each line are the abbreviations for the twelve months of the year.

58. Fill the Blank
The number is seven.

59. Do You Deny It?
The word is "deny."

60. Where to Draw the Lines?
IN/DISC/RIM/IN/AT/I/ON

61. He! He!
The word HEADACHE answers both questions.

62. Guess the Punchlines
1. BOYFRIEND: May I see it?
2. WAITER: There was, but I wiped it off.
3. STUDENT: At the bottom.
4. PRISONER: I'll have a ham sandwich.
5. PSYCHIATRIST: Next!
6. DOCTOR: That's what puzzles me.
7. PATIENT: Well, yes and no.

63. The Wrong Words
The rooms were marked *Ladies* and *Gentlemen*.

64. A Typewriter Teaser
Typewriter.

65. Professor Letterman's Revenge
He erased the l of *lasses*.

66. The Marrying Bachelor
Tim Rines is the MINISTER of the First EPISCOPAL Church.

67. HIJKLMNO
H to O or H_2O, the chemical symbol for water — two atoms of hydrogen combined with one atom of oxygen.

68. An Unusual Word
Unusual.

69. A Clock Conundrum
IV (ivy).

70. Ten Body Parts
Arm, leg, ear, toe, lip, hip, eye, rib, jaw, gum.

71. Opposites

G	R	O	W
R	I	P	E
O	P	E	N
W	E	N	T

(Tim Tebbe contributed this to *Games* magazine.)

72. ERGRO
UNDERGROUND.

73. One-Letter Captions
J (jay), Q (queue), I (eye), B (bee), T (cup of tea), P (pea), C (sea), U (mirror — you).

74. The Annoyed Sign Painter
He changed the sign to THE BELLYACHE COMPANY.

75. Fold and Cut
Believe it or not, the *only* word you can make is HEAD. (Thanks to magician Max Maven for this one.)

76. In and Out
1. exist.
2. blank.
3. center.

77. From Z to A
The word ZEBRA.

78. What Can It Be?
The letter L.

79. Number Anagram
One, Ten, and Six.

80. ENINYOS
Ten tiny tots.

81. Name the Painting
The Mona Lisa.

82. The Locked Safe
Psyche.

83. Change the Sign
Private?
No! Swimming Allowed

84. Three B's

The word is "hubbub."

85. Horace Spencer

"My age twelve years, height four feet ten, sir."

86. What's the Number?

One.

87. NY, PA, AND OZ

Shift each letter of OZ one step backward in the alphabet and you get NY. Shift the letters of OZ forward one step (assuming a circular alphabet in which Z is joined to A) and you get PA.

88. Curious Cards

Mr. Curio changes the word to N-O-P-E.

89. GHGHGH

The word is *puff.*

90. HAL and IBM

Shift the letters of HAL forward one step in the alphabet. They become IBM. Clarke claims that this was sheer coincidence. He never intended HAL to shift to IBM.

91. Ten Flying Saucers

Shift each letter of TEN one step forward in the alphabet and it becomes UFO.

92. Kubla Khan

In each line the last two main words begin with the same letter. Critics call this "alliteration."

93. Merry Christmas

Not only do the first words of each line repeat the words of the first line, but the same line is repeated by taking the first word of the first line, second word of the second line, third word of the third line, and so on to the end.

94. Two Words
The x word is *drive*, and the y word is *park*.

95. Blind Bus Driver
The "Blind Man" is the owner of a company that sells window blinds.

96. A Lewis Carroll Puzzle
BIG FACED. In an 1877 letter Lewis Carroll gave this word teaser to Maud Stanton, one of his many child friends.

97. A Curious Sequence
The next pair is also TH. They are the last two letters of FIRST, SECOND, THIRD, FOURTH, and FIFTH.

98. Name Two
Dwarf, dwell, and dwindle.

99. Decode a Number
Eighty-four.

100. Miles and Miles
Smiles, smiled, smiler, and smiley.

101. After AB
E comes after AB in "alphabet."

102. Add a Line
ABODE.

103. The End. Have a good day.

ABOUT THE AUTHOR

World famous as the puzzle master who wrote the "Mathematical Games" column of *Scientific American* magazine for 25 years, Martin Gardner has also written close to 70 books on such subjects as science (including a book that *Time* magazine called "by far the most lucid explanation of Einstein's theories"), mathematics, philosophy, religion, poetry, literary criticism (including *The Annotated Alice*, a classic examination of *Alice in Wonderland* that is still selling large numbers of copies now, more than 30 years after it was first published), and, of course, puzzles (out of 29 puzzle books for adults and children, only one is out of print!).

The son of an Oklahoma wildcat oil prospector, Gardner attended the University of Chicago, where he received a degree in philosophy. After graduation he worked on the *Tulsa* (Oklahoma) *Tribune*. He sold his first story to *Esquire*, published articles on logic and math in specialist magazines, and became a contributing editor to *Humpty Dumpty's Magazine* before starting his legendary column.

Martin Gardner has had a lifelong passion for conjuring, and many of his original magic tricks have become classics among magicians.

Dubbed "The Magician of Math" by *Newsweek*, Gardner, now retired, makes his home in North Carolina, where he continues to amaze his fans with more and more books, articles, and ideas.

INDEX